false anatomy

selected poems by kate soupiset

2014-2019

FIRST PRINTING—APRIL, 2019
SOUPCAN PRESS
SAN ANTONIO, TEXAS, USA

false

ISBN: 9781095082737
Copyright ©2019 Kate Soupiset. All Rights Reserved.
Published with Kindle Direct Publishing by Soupcan Press.

anatomy

To my father; to my teacher, Mr. Cruz,
and to anyone else who has ever made me write
—you are the reason this exists

To my mother, and every educator
—you are our nation's greatest treasure

part one
because we are flawless

False Anatomy

a ceramic woman
dustless in a dusty museum
armless, yet armed
with an ideal visage and chest
curved and preserved
for eyes
young and unblinking

did she really exist, though,
as she appears under this spotlight
did she exist
how this glossy, airbrushed woman
exists in this magazine, this billboard, this screen?

I am not Venus
I am not Kim
and neither are you

statues
screens
easily crack
these representations don't represent

What I'd Like To Believe

First off
I'd like to believe
he didn't die
didn't die so young

He didn't make plans
past September 21
the day the waters of this world
claimed him

Could he feel it? Did he know?

I'd like to believe he didn't get excited for his thirteenth
birthday
didn't have a crush
didn't think about what was for dinner
didn't think of who he could be
what he could do
didn't wonder what the world had to offer him.

Did he feel God pulling him from the Earth?
traveling the distance to heaven?
uprooting his life?
separating spirit from body?

Could he feel that the world
didn't have much left to give him?
His friends didn't have much left to say?
His parents were okay with
him slipping through their fingers?

But he couldn't, could he?

carpet burn

I do not breathe
but creep
on hands and knees
like a hungry animal
my sister
my sidekick
her cautious breaths
crawl from her mouth
and spill silently onto the floor

we dare not make a sound
louder than the air conditioning's
soft hums and whispers
for it is early

not the alarm
not the bright sunshine
not the hummingbirds outside the window
not this old house's occasional exhale
but us
we will be the ones to wake them

Naïve

I wished I could've stayed there forever
buried in a castle
of blue pillows
I was quiet
I was dense
I was still
nothing in the world could shake me
at least, at age six,
nothing I knew of

only the light that
impaled me
through holes
in my castle walls
could halt my breathing

but I wouldn't let it.

from a mailbox to a bird

my love
I wait
for you
to stop

wait for you
to give me
all you have
to let me
hold your love
every last word

They say I'm bad
at keeping secrets but
I'll try my best
for me and you

Now take me with you
steal me from the sidewalk
no one could stop us

I love you more than stamps.

Morning

A rabbit crawls out of his earthy home
You wake to thunder
He jogs to the lake and back
A bee meets the day's first flower
the sprinklers click on *ch-ch-ch-ch*
She wakes up not knowing where she is
He now realizes he wasn't falling
She's home from work and ready for sleep
The daughter spends two hours in front of the mirror
A leaf gently kisses the grass below
The wind is here to climb down throats
An egg falls from a nest
The bus driver speeds
The student types the final word of his essay: cooperation.
He wakes up with butterflies
The sun peeks over the hill, glimpsing at the landscape.
Nothing has changed.
God blinks.

gold.

I push you away with the force
of a pen
gallons of ink
tons of paper
I search my room for a journal
to write this poem in
and I realize
you have scattered yourself
throughout the house
in slips of paper
in echoes of songs I don't even like

and here I am.
embedding you into yet another artifact
to be dug up a time from now
hopefully when I have answers
or know what went wrong

I'll find you here
a memory
or a dream

I spent the summer
forgetting you
thought you wouldn't exist anymore
just a memory

and here we are
early September
same as always
you didn't even get taller

every song sounds like you

A Warning

don't talk to me
because if you talk to me
you'll get stuck in my head
shelved among annoying songs
and today's quiz answers

don't get stuck in my head
if you get stuck in my head
you'll get stuck in my heart
seated between my family and friends

don't get stuck in my heart
if you get stuck in my heart
you'll get stuck in my hands
needles pulling thread
knitting, knitting, knitting

don't get stuck in my hands
if you get stuck in my hands
you'll get stuck in my poems
the office I visit for therapy
the cave I retire to for breathing
and my poems
are the most permanent destination
of all.

Good Medicine

sleep is good for a cluttered mind
writing is helpful during heartbreak
cats cure loneliness
beaches mend a wandering heart

apologies for broken promises
sad songs for sad days
socks for cold feet
rainy days for unread books

lipstick for monotonous mornings
secrets for dull friendships
boys for boredom
feminism for the patriarchy

glasses for nearsightedness
bridges for chasms
listening for lack of understanding
hands for a broken world

Back to Neighborly

i
I don't know my neighbors
I've never seen them
only cars in front of houses
only noises over fences

They used to all talk
everyone was so social
everyone was friendly
no one was lonely
no one was afraid to speak.

ii
The movie theatre is filled
with people
but empty seats are visible
between each person.

The bar is lined up with malts and coffees
but blue light separates
barista from customer.

The line for the food truck
is twenty heads long
but no eyes align
to meet in friendly conversation.

The stories my grandparents tell me
make me wonder
what it was like
to know thy neighbor
to love thy neighbor
to be loved by thy neighbor

Snapshot

Invisible spells
spill from my mouth
My hands are clasped
making a mountain range of knuckles
I can feel my eyes
moving behind
shades made from skin

I talk to Nicholas
drifting in a dream
then reality throws rocks
at my stiff body
my words stick to my teeth
my sweaty hands become maracas
but a deep breath
plunges me back

The front wheel is like the bow of a vessel,
clearing way for my transportation
I look down and notice the back of my hand,
curved around the handle bars.
running down the back of it are two gray rivers
I look back past the bow
to see I'm headed for a ditch.
swerve.
The bow tilts sideways and collapses
The rivers slacken their grip on
the handle bars and break my fall
the asphalt is familiar
I'm bleeding.

I lie half-awake
too lazy to look at the clock
My mind turns in my skull,
realizes my hands are empty shelves
As I sink into the cotton waves of sleep,
I remember what it feels like to be alone.

blood poem

on my way to the airport
I remembered the sheets
I had left them stained—
my personal seal on my cousin's bedding—
never actually got the chance to look

here's the poem for closure.
that's how I tend to leave things
with ink and blood.

Whispers

Because we are girls
Because we are bored
Because gossip is water and we are thirsty
Because it's past midnight
Because I'm always a good girl
Because we are flawless, and their lives are more interesting than ours
Because we felt invincible
Because we see their cracks, when we think we are spotless windows

Anatomy Lesson

Every time I shake
a new freckle grows
My hair is like
Pinocchio's nose
and it's long.
My nose is irrelevant
My mouth is a mystery.

Let's travel down the trachea
Explore my lungs and veins
Take a turn to the heart

It smells like smashed china
and breathes like mountain air
I can remember the taste
crayons without names and sand

My feet kiss the icy concrete
I'm stupid to not wear shoes
But I don't care
Fusion, as I am tropical and it is arctic

In my brain
there are no neurons
no lobes
only thoughts
that clutter like a growing cobweb

The lunch lady serves me
voices
My face is just a façade
on the inside
I'm really screaming
at the ceiling fan.

part two
*because if the
momentum of
eyelids falling*

Slow Down

On a sidewalk, wide enough for one,
were two.
Her shiny ponytail swung
in a bouncy rhythm
from left to right
a pendulum
a countdown.
His big shirt rubbed up against her.

On a sidewalk, wide enough for one,
were two
Their synchronized steps
almost overlapped in discomfort
Walk a little faster
The metronome of blond hair ticked faster.

On a sidewalk wide enough for one
were two
one falling behind the other.
The sun shone like the gleaming jewel
of a wedding ring.
Her swaying hair
was the long, flared shape
of a college diploma.
The wind whispered, grow up

He called after her,
Slow down

Island Candy

Seafoam green boards
stacked up
wilting in the coastal humidity

selling sweet things
for salty people
rattlesnake in a cage
just like these island people

I was a patron to the wrong cause
racist signs covered the walls
I didn't even notice
until she told me on the bus ride home
"There was a Trump sign above the register."

Horrified, I ate my island candy
in shame.

Haircut

To Jessica,
who snipped away
10 inches
10 inches of thoughts
long tendrils of consideration
hanging from my head
I like to wear my cluttered-mindedness
10 inches of worry
the hair that weighed me down
dragged at my feet
collected dirt: insecurities, bad habits and rudeness
like a broom
10 inches of waiting
10 months of hell
10 friends built a wall around this hair
so I chopped it
well, Jessica did
got rid of the twisted tracks on which
my train of thought traveled
only kept the feeling
mostly sad, confused and stuck
10 inches dead
but reincarnated.

Wake Up

it's ten til two am.
who the hell's awake?
the dreamers are awake
the writers are awake
the romantics are awake
the person with something to say is awake
because if the momentum of eyelids falling
can send their minds deep down under the waves of
consciousness
they could forget
forgetting
a dreamer's worst enemy
I can't forget this feeling:
blissful ignorance
I've convinced myself that I'm untouchable
you're attainable
nothing is crazy
I can say anything
I can't forget
so I'm writing it down

I'm awake with all of
the eccentric thinkers
trying not to forget.

So join us.
Wake up.

Filling

He is a true mirror
showing me the beauty
I refuse to notice

He separates tangles into three sections
braids them into an answer
he takes my scattered ingredients
insecurity, curiosity, empathy
and bakes them into dough
he offers me this sweet something
to make my stomach full

We exchange chips
from our cracked clay hearts
our pieces filling each other's holes

Run To Me

when sleep has taped your eyes open
and unhinged your mind
when all the light
inside and out
has gone
when you start thinking of her
when you're scared you won't
be able to
give her the care she deserves
when you imagine losing her

let your tears hit the blue screen
but run to me in your mind
knowing
that all of your problems are temporary
and that the love will run out
of some faster than others

and I'll build walls to keep you safe
until they are weathered away
by the winds and waves
of all the people that
you'll meet
someday
I'll leave you
someday
someone new
will lay a brick at your gates
because you are
a treasure worth protecting

Respite

my voice crawls out from underneath
our arms and clothes

"It doesn't matter"
she whispers

It might be the chemicals in my body
I don't think it's just school
It might be my infidelity to God

"It doesn't matter"
she whispers

She pulls me down
from dark to darker
wraps her arms around me

my eyes, fixed on the gray light
falling through the navy blinds

I implode
crumble in on myself

breathe in my mother's heartbeat

Worn Thin
Inspired by "Metaphor and the Authenticating
Act of Memory" by Stephen Dobyns

i.
the thick man with thin skin
is pinned
to the sheets he thinks he can fade into
he forgets how his soul is

ii.
A raven
A beetle's back
the smoke floating from a burning house
his great great grandfather's top hat
worn past its tenure
the cold, metal shell
of a typewriter
its keys pressed
He is a glass prism.

iii.
he supposes afternoon naps will cure him
he believes that gravity's power will soon fulfill its purpose
and plunge him down
into those sheets
suffocate him in escapism
where he can hide forever

iv.
he'll never have to come out
not for meetings or parties or concerts or soccer games or
weddings
maybe if God tugs at his sleeve hard enough
he'll sneak out from behind the curtain
at least for a little while

Curriculum

I. Echoes of Identity

She played songs without any commentary. Let the words wash over us. She taught me to be okay with my doubts. She taught me to never give up on the people I love in my life, until the miles become too far to stretch my heart. She taught me how independence can be a weapon. I always look at her through kaleidoscopes, see her fragments multiplied into patterns. She is never a sharp photograph or a straight line. She is always bended light and blended color. But now she has moved away. Smaller in my field of vision. Thousands of small big sisters staring back at me. Thousands of replications of who I know her to be. She has moved away and I have stretched myself over the distance and I can still love her. After a sisterhood of misunderstandings, borrowed clothes, confusion and car rides, I finally start to understand who she is and who she is meant to be.

II. Misunderstood

It's not that she couldn't learn the curriculum, it's that the curriculum couldn't learn her. She always seemed to be one step behind, one degree slanted, one connection short. She never climbed as far up the ladder as the rest of us did. To the teachers she was an empty hole. To me she was a question mark. To God she was a lightbulb. Eleven years of feeling not good enough can damage a person's spirit. Eleven years of almost drowning, just keeping her eyes above the surface. After eleven years, when their ears tuned into what our family was trying to say, they gave her a test. Then they gave her medicine. Then they gave her the tests that had mocked her. Then she made her first A.

III. Distance is Relative

I always knew she loved me, but she never showed me. She wouldn't give me hugs, wouldn't talk much at all to me. I got lost in her unique way of expression. But after a sisterhood of sharing clothes, a room, and a year of car rides to school accompanied by her unexplained playlists, I felt like she knew I knew she loved me. Eleven years a floorboard away. Three years a bathroom away. Two months 143 miles away. She visited the other weekend. She showed me the paintings she has completed and the ones she is working on. She bought a keyboard and can play more chords than me. She said college isn't fun. She briefly told me about the one friend she made. She talked more about the past than the present. Now I see her through a phone. I see her in her bedroom, in her kitchen, in a classroom, in a car, in a Whataburger. I see her on the top of a cliff, sunrise behind her, saying goodbye to her best friend. She is still bended light and blended color. I still see her indirectly. But now I see her overwhelming beauty.

Sound It Out

i.
sound waves become glue
filling the gaps in my heart the best it can
repeat the words until I believe them
you're stupid you're stupid you're stupid

ii.
when these songs play
I hear my father's voice
in the places where harmony should be
over tornadoes, oceans and Babylon

iii.
it's the potter
that changes the expressions of my face
makes me dance in the mirror, carefree
lights the match in my soul

iv.
better than any speech
than any photo album
than any painting
the melody says what I've been trying to

v.
it makes me feel like I've been here before
except I haven't
like when you know a beautiful place
only by its postcards

vi.
always playing in the back of my head
the last thing that leaves us before death
glues our voices together
keeps us sane, keeps us compassionate

Like a Wheelbarrow over Gravel
Starting with a line from Mary Oliver

to live in this world
what an extreme request

to live in this world
where tongues aren't long enough
to lick
I feel most alive
in stillness

where God nudges me forward
like a wheelbarrow over gravel

how could I live in this world

Untethered
After Louise Glück

Is it summer again, is it hot again
are we here again, talking in your backyard
didn't you hurt me again
with words, not the choking kind,
the ones that soil my throat

didn't you clump together
at the edge of the pool
like a bunch of geese

didn't my throat clench
didn't my heart contract
wasn't I happy once—

I remember the sun bothering me
to play with him
but the shade's wind had a softer whisper

wasn't I gifted with twelve sisters
ones to play with my hair
ones to sing me songs
ones to pray over the life
I haven't lived—

haven't I lived
in the peace and friendliness of others

aren't people good
aren't friends nice
don't you love me
can't you see I'm trying

as the light bulbs shatter once more
and the wind comes again to chill
won't you love me now?

Lamentation for the Laurels

the rain came last night
made all the colors of everything
bleed and blend
together in a painter's haze

the rain brought the wind with it
and the wind
it screamed and yelled at the trees
until they were forced
to bend and lean and fall
making the roofs into their beds

then morning came
and the trees had no leaves to give the sun
and the mountain laurels cried their last
and the people came out
to see what damage was done

Quitting Time

That mid-morning saw the desolation of the honeybees
high in their tree, fit together tight, their hive
a geode, the chaos, the beauty hidden within
a working buzz, a hum to move them along
then they were met with the drip drip drop
of insecticide

Shift

As it takes time
for leaves to fall
so it does
for the fingernails to grow
for the pictures to get lost in my drawer
for the christmas lights to be packed away in green boxes

I wonder if
our calendars
are just engines
we need to choke out and stall
standing a moment
on the railroads of stillness
or are they
rulers
measuring
how long it takes for us to let go

There is a beauty I find in waves
they will return with certainty
to the shore
bringing new ocean each time
safety and wonder, married on a beach

Similarly, my waves have returned each month
between my legs
without fail
thirty-nine times
the first tide flooded me
but I've since learned
how to tread in my own water

When You Ask Me How I'm Doing

I won't mention the dying flowers
in my kitchen window
or the new stones in my backyard
marking where I buried my cat
in September

I won't talk about how different you look
nails cut short
hair grown long
how your face is more shadow than light

I won't let you know
how many times I've thought of you
since June
how God is a memory
and you are a scar

Lullaby

In the early days we stared at you, I stared at you, with equal parts confusion and wonder. Your true nature came to me piece by piece, note by note. We made you a part of the family, nurtured your layers. We watched you grow up, mature into the music you are, fill the dots and lines on the page with substance. Last week I realized how you've begun to crack and whimper and sigh. I noticed the age in your rests.

Tonight we brought you out and dusted you off. We played you how you were meant to be. We touched all the smooth spots and felt your punches when our bows scratched against the strings with ferocity. In the madness I heard your message. I heard the love in a mother's voice, the sweet hushing of a midnight sky. You are the gentle hands that clasp around calamity and chaos and from it produce peace and delight.

Tomorrow we bury you. We pull you out from our veins and place you before the world. We reveal your sound to ears who have never tasted your tune. We play you with confidence and the right number of mistakes, one last time. And when the time comes for the strings to unhinge themselves from their wooden braces, and wrap themselves tightly around my neck, I will say goodbye to you last with six sweet short words.

And just like that you are a piece of memory.

part three

*because it's not
about this weekend*

A sickness, an illness
After Maurice Manning

have you ever gotten sick Boss do you
know how it feels Boss when your stomach
hurts a good illness Boss a good illness have
you ever been in love I think I might be in love Boss
the hair is nice and the mouth laughs
when it thinks I'm being funny Boss how
do I say I love you how do I tell
the eyes they are beautiful when should
I say I love you help Boss I want to show
you my heart in here but it's broken Boss
and you've never been great at fixing things
Boss how did you fall in love how did you
tell the hair, eyes, hands how beautifully
they danced and slept and lived together
Boss I think I'm in love

Ars Poetica
Inspired by the work of Archibald MacLeish

Poetry is a source of life
like the sun to the earth

Poetry is God on paper
unclear if she owns the words she writes

Poetry is music
voice of the quiet, finding sound in dark splotches

Poetry is the city
alive behind the hardware store counter

Poetry is all the quiet places in the world
cowering from loud noises

Poetry is all the white, bearded men
writing by lamplight on ornate, wooden desks

Poetry is her white dresses
and inability to name her work

Poetry is the cave we return to
nocturnal words slipping from our heads

epistle

I just wanted to let you know
that she has lost most of your confidence
and none of your humor

still wears your bright smile
but differently now
like how you have to work to keep the waves from flooding
your sandcastle

likes to dance
like you do
but only in the comfort of her own room
or in the company of the people who will dance with her

taller than the boys
wider than the girls
losing the blondeness in her hair
finding the redness in her face

she still goes through boys like you both go through books
very, very slowly

Thinks more
of herself
of others
of god
of the world

She asks even more questions than you do, impossible as it
may seem.

I just wanted to let you know
that it's okay to be loud
you can cry anytime
you're allowed to whine
because you need to
I want you to love yourself like she should now

She told me you should spend more time with your brother
and father
and that things with your sister get so much better
and you might not realize it now
but you're pretty friendless
and friends, my dear, will be the best gift of growing up

perhaps a wall

The moon has come to save me
scoop me into its craters and zoom back out of focus

The land
rimose
the people
on fire

a split seam
the two sides of a dam
a fault line
the continental divide

I can't seem to climb any of these mountains
so I'll have to fall
into something less than earth
a hole in a rock in the sky

Glacial Fantasy

Would you be so kind
as to run away with me
down an unknown beaten path
to anywhere but here
leaving our problems
flaws
behind
in a secret cave underground
among the bats
pinch-faced and whiney
who eat away at them every single day,
the sweet sticky blackness clinging to their teeth,
in their dark home
that drips secrets from the ceiling
or we can sink our doubts in the ocean
with the weight of our fears
and let them swim past the places the light touches
past the place where life lives
to rest on the darkest sand
or we can stuff our questions in a wooden box
and tie a shiny navy balloon around it
and let it float into the sky
until the wood, rubber and string themselves
become one of the stars
we can look up and see
from our new
latitude
longitude
home
?

I pray for the woman ahead of me
in the H-E-B checkout line

I see her unkempt wavy brown hair
her tall body dressed in black
then her red nail polish
fingers and toes
then the bottle of wine on the conveyor belt
then the pack of cigarettes the store clerk
pulls from the cabinet with slow fingers

I pray for her safety tonight
I pray for what she's trying to forget
or remember
what she lost
or what she found

Then I think how righteous I feel
that's it
pity, empathy to the point of self-recognition
I am her
I want to ask her to
share my doughnut with me

Amen.

Public Storage
After O'Hara and John

Scratches appear on my arms
unannounced
my clothes are lumpy
hell, I'm lumpy
curves and bumps arrive
without fanfare, or even a heads-up
to compensate for all I'm
storing inside
the license plates and the swing sets
the punchlines and the questions
I'm just a garage
used to hoard
all the problems and joys and knowledge of the world
I will try to figure you out
I will try gather your trinkets and tchotchkes
so leave your treasures on the front porch.

Ode To Moving On

This ode has been sleeping in a damp hull of a ship
somewhere in my chest
the weekend a hurricane
my body never saw the eye

The ode decided to stir
realized it was his time to take the stage
sooner or later
he's waiting in the wings
waiting for me to move out of the damn spotlight

Because it's not about this weekend
it's not about this ephemeral moment
it's about what comes next
Exit left.

Enter MOVING ON.
Behind the curtains I watch him
deceive the audience—
deception... I know the feeling
being in control
on the top of a mountain
behind a podium
and then suddenly you're falling through the floor
the ceiling
the floor—
Everything is okay.
He is a magician
the world: wide-eyed children
his sleight of hand tricks aren't that good
people are just that dumb.
"Look behind your ear
there's her smile
look under your chair
there's her warm hug."

he takes a bow

but his time isn't up
there must be more he can do
then I see his dark eyes turn my way
Exit left.

"Now it's your turn.
Time for you to see what it's all about."
He casts a spell over me
nothing hurts
nothing stings
Nothing.

He tells me to get up and walk.
I laugh.
He tells me I'm healed.
I get up and walk.
But where?
"Away."

Unrequited
with lines from "Paper-Thin Hotel" by Leonard Cohen

I've spent the summer swimming
at first it wasn't quite a sport
more a tactic for survival
to keep from drowning

next I let myself sink
opened my eyes
let the salt come burn them
let the pain come ruin

now I find myself floating
I've forgiven the water
and now I rest upon what it's become

and as the sun burns my skin red
and while you dive in all your own
my heartbeat is the sound of piano chords

a heavy burden lifted from my soul
I heard that love was out of my control

Sandwich Shop at 8 p.m.

I am alone
in the sandwich shop
at a table for two
texting my friend a joke
about how I'm on a date
like a normal girl my age should be
on a Friday night

I notice
a bald head
hunched over, staring ahead into the distance
unaware that I've been staring
his blue shirt
with red little stars
reminds me of something or someone

and as he crumples up his wrapper
and adjusts his glasses
and clasps his hands, almost prayerfully,
he doesn't know—can't know—
he's made me feel
purposeful
tonight.

Getting a Grip

I grope in the dark
my blind, restless hand
waving, silent but urgent
urgent to speak

my hand lands on a shoulder
in front of me
a shoulder is enough

I tell that shoulder everything
my nails digging in deeper
with each parting of my lips

I only stop to breathe
when I have nothing left to say
when I'm dry
when all the words have been pushed out of me

and a hand grabs my shoulder
with conviction and comfort
our arms form a bridge

It is outside myself
but it holds me still

Someday I'll Love Kate Soupiset
After Frank O'Hara

the mumbler
the overthinker
the faller
she has her perks

someday she'll stop worrying
and just take a walk
someday her head will fall quiet
and she'll lie down in a stream
and let the clear, cool water rush over her skin

someday she will remember whose
shoulders she's standing on
whose money is in her wallet
whose blood is in her veins

someday she'll just stand still
let the world move around her
until she knows its speed and joins the race
that's the day I will love her

Banana Pancakes *Kind of Happy*

I slouch away from the restaurant
towards my car
a chest full of mud

when suddenly from behind me
a man in a Jeep
the kind without windows or doors
rolls up beside me
blasting "Banana Pancakes"
singing out loud
one leg hanging out the side
a Christmas bow on the hood

no clouds in the reflection of his sunglasses
no one in the passenger seat
only a grin
its shadow stretching over onto the asphalt

inside my Buick
I queue up the same song
the empty seats fill with music

Girl (All The Way Down)

foot on the brake pedal
lips chapped
blood slides between the cracks
lives in her bed
in her desk
in her car

eyes on glass
sentences short
the music in her head
churns, fuels.
the watch on her wrist
is a metaphor

she wants to press the gas pedal
all the way down
with her big feet
she wants to speak oceans
with her small lips
she craves beauty at midnight
with her full stomach
she is running
life on her feet
life in the world
everytime she closes her eyes

Made in the USA
Las Vegas, NV
15 December 2022

62811735R00038